Being Responsible

by Robin Nelson

first step nonfiction

Lerner Publications Company · Minneapolis

I am **responsible.**

I do what I am supposed
to do.

I am responsible at home.

I put my toys away.

I take care of my dog.

I help my brother.

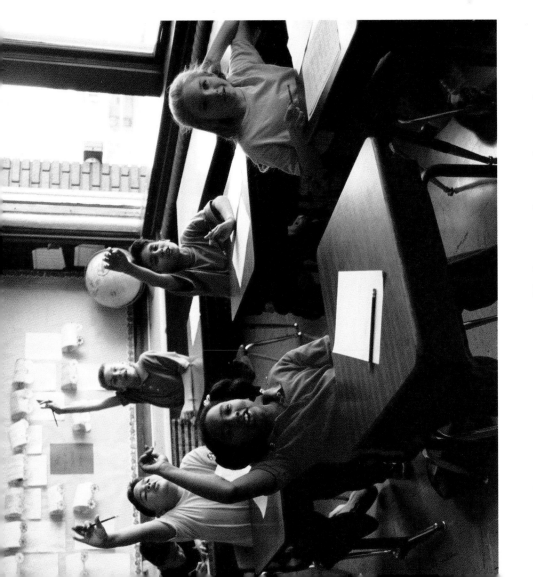

I am responsible at school.

I turn in my homework.

I follow **directions.**

I work hard.

I am responsible in my **community.**

I follow rules.

I help others.

I do not **litter.**

Being responsible makes me
feel good about myself.

Being responsible makes me feel **proud.**

How can you be responsible at home?

- Tell the truth.

- Feed your pet.

- Hang up your coat.

- Tell your parents when you do something wrong.

- Look out for your younger brother or sister.

How can you be responsible at school?

- Throw away your trash.

- Do not blame others for something you did.

- Always do your best.

- Turn in your homework on time.

- Listen to your teacher.

Glossary

community – the area where a group of people live

directions – things that tell you how to do something

litter – to leave trash around

proud – happy about something you did

responsible – having a job to do; trustworthy